Nationwide Nightmare

Nationwide Nightmare

Orion Ember

CONTENTS

Introduction 1

1 Chapter 1: Early Life and Development of Israel Ke 4

2 Chapter 2: Keyes' Modus Operandi 7

3 Chapter 3: The First Known Murders 10

4 Chapter 4: Unraveling the Mystery 13

5 Chapter 5: The Hunt for Additional Victims 16

6 Chapter 6: The Shocking Revelation of Murder Cache 18

7 Chapter 7: Keyes' Legacy and Impact 20

8 Chapter 8: Lessons Learned and Future Implications 23

Conclusion 26

Appendix: Keyes' Known Victims and Timeline 28

Bibliography 30

Copyright © 2025 by Orion Ember
All rights reserved. No part of this book may be reproduced in any manner whatsoever without written permission except in the case of brief quotations embodied in critical articles and reviews.
First Printing, 2025

Introduction

This book is a true story, grounded in countless hours of meticulous research on the case and Israel Keyes himself. Unlike other true crime books, such as *American Predator*, this one delves deep into the enigmatic world of Israel Keyes: his background, crimes, upbringing, family, children, and a behind-the-scenes look at his relationships with certain individuals. It also details the tragic discovery of Samantha Koenig, shedding light on the dark origins of a killer who initially seemed to have none.

By sharing exclusive details that only media outlets have glimpsed, such as his chilling suicide note, I aim to unlock at least a portion of the secrets that Keyes may have taken to his grave. *Nationwide Nightmare: The True Story of Israel Keyes and His Murder Caches* is a compelling exploration of the life of Israel Keyes, a killer who confessed to multiple brutal murders across the United States. What sets his case apart is his eerie claim: he'd buried murder caches in numerous locations, committing burglaries, bank robberies, and lootings over the years. He believed the FBI would never connect him to these crimes. Unlike other accounts, this book focuses on Keyes himself rather than the lives and deaths of each victim.

Background of Israel Keyes

Israel Keyes was born on January 7, 1978, in Richmond, Utah, into a family of Mormon fundamentalists. Married at 18, he and his wife moved frequently, thanks to his military service. Keyes was trained in psychological operations—essentially the art of negotiation and persuasion. He briefly attended engineering school but dropped out. His formative years were marked by instability; as a teenager, he frequently got into trouble for burglarizing homes. He and his wife were deeply involved in the neo-Nazi group Aryan Nations for seven years until they left in 2000.

Given all Keyes had witnessed and experienced, he might have grown disillusioned with the world—or at least his version of it. His psychological operations training made him adept at getting people to trust him and open their homes to him. Despite this, robbery alone never seemed to provide enough of a thrill. Keyes often spoke of a need to do things that no one else had done, a desire for control over his actions, and an ability to "hide in the shadows." These aspects of his personality certainly contributed to his terrifying spree.

Purpose and Scope of the Book

The purpose of this book is to provide a detailed narrative of Israel Keyes' crimes and travels, organized by the zones in which he primarily operated. This structure allows readers to discern between known and unknown aspects of his criminal activity and develop a sense of time and space relative to his crimes. My hope is that this narrative will be a useful representation of the known details, gaps, and unanswered questions surrounding Israel Keyes.

For instance, on the weekend of February 5, 2011, Keyes traveled to four states, including Montana. However, information about incidents in these states is either unknown or publicly undocumented. This book takes readers on a zone-by-zone journey through a selection of countries, states, cities, and towns frequented by Keyes. It includes a look at his travels during each season and estimates the time he spent at or near each location. Possible disparate crimes have been included to show the breadth of his activity.

To further emphasize the extent of Keyes' reach, a list of known cities and towns for his international travel is included. However, the lack of specific information about his international trips, such as exact addresses, has made a more thorough season-by-season exploration impossible. My hope is that this work raises interest in the described locations and brings some levity and tranquility to all areas connected to Israel Keyes. May we continue to keep the dark victims found at each location in our hearts.

Chapter 1: Early Life and Development of Israel Ke

Young Israel (1986-1992)

Israel Keyes was born in Richmond, Utah, in January of 1978, during a snowstorm in the family station wagon. He was the fifth of ten children, and his early life was fraught with challenges. His mother, Heidi, was only 18 years old when she had him, and by the time she was 28, she had ten children. Israel quickly assumed the role of "chief babysitter."

The Keyes family initially lived in two rooms behind Heidi's grandparents' house before moving eight miles away to their own modest home in the "boonies." Life at the Keyes compound was never idle—there were always livestock to tend, fences to repair, and wood to chop.

In 1986, Ted, Israel's father, abruptly announced that he was moving to Oregon with two of the children, leaving the rest of the family in Utah. Israel, right in the middle of the nine siblings, showed exceptional skill and bravery, taking care of the animals, chopping wood, and even attempting to bake cakes with corn oil. During these tumultuous times, the family fell under the influence of the Church of Jesus Christ of Latter-day Saints, a force for good that they embraced for decades.

CHAPTER 1: EARLY LIFE AND DEVELOPMENT OF ISRAEL KE

Family Background and Childhood

Israel Keyes was born on January 7, 1978, in Cove, Utah. His father, a power technician, lost his job when the energy company he worked for went out of business. The family owned land in Utah, where Israel's grandmother's brother and uncle also lived. When Israel was about five, his younger sister, Ariel, was diagnosed with cancer. Despite the family's efforts, she passed away on March 25, 1987. This tragic event deeply impacted Israel, who became morbidly fascinated with fires, seemingly in search of death.

The Keyes family moved several times before settling in the Colville Valley by the 1980s. They lived at 1944 Deep Lake Boundary Road and found a community with the Trinity Bible Church. Israel was intelligent and motivated but also impulsive and antisocial. He showed early signs of psychopathic traits, withdrawing from social interactions and displaying antisocial behavior. According to Robert Pickton, Keyes "didn't socialize and no one really talked to him."

Signs of Disturbance and Isolation

Israel Keyes was a morose outlier from the beginning, the product of an unstable family. Born on January 7, 1978, in Richmond, Utah, he was always a misfit. As a listless college freshman, he stood out as grim and reclusive among his peers at Michigan's Ogemaw Heights High School. Keyes had a sarcastic and nihilistic streak, often posting dark and poetic statuses on Facebook.

At 15, he felt isolated and creative in a way that others couldn't understand. He was deeply affected by acquiring the James Fenimore Cooper novel *Deerslayer* at the age of 12, a gift from his grandparents. Though creative, Keyes was a loner, preferring to play indoors due to his severe allergic reaction to the sun and heat.

In the moose capital of Michigan, Keyes adopted a secluded lifestyle. According to local Jack Pearce, "Just about everyone in town was on food stamps. You have to remember the culture of a child in that town—growing up on an outdoors saturation of pristine lakes and hauntingly huge moose doesn't excite him much. That was just him."

Chapter 2: Keyes' Modus Operandi

Modus Operandi
Before Israel Keyes arrived in Anchorage, his method for disposing of "kill kits" was straightforward: burn them. Initially, they intended to burn the Vermouth Dr. Pepper box Keyes carried into the shed. The huge metal drum with holes drilled over the top would quickly incinerate the ropes, Keyes explained. However, Keyes also brought kits without ropes that he deemed suitable for export and proposed dissolving the remaining ones in Druch's tubs of acid. It quickly became clear to both of them which ropeless kits would be traveling and which would dissolve in acid. "There was a noticeable difference in presenting themselves," Druch said, "like, 'These could be moving. These are a problem.'"

Though Keyes didn't specify his methods that day, investigators would eventually uncover an intricate operation. Each part was deliberate but not necessarily methodical. While each abduction was unique, there were patterns: He avoided abducting people he knew personally but wouldn't hesitate to grab an acquaintance or someone he was familiar with. He studied his subject's schedules and mannerisms, planning the abduction to make it seem like they disappeared suddenly. Keyes, slightly ambidextrous, preferred his subjects to face away from him. He knew his passengers were bracing for a crash scene, which gave him the invaluable element of surprise. Keyes' attention to detail allowed him to psychologically manipulate his victims. He drilled locks, checked for alarm systems, and buried his kits in light vegetation where forestry fires were common. Each cache contained what Keyes would need for opportunistic crimes. He could either kill easily or stage a drowning if he didn't feel like murdering, which is why investigators found float tanks on several bodies.

Travel and Preparation

The most notable aspect of Keyes' bank robberies was the amount of time he spent preparing for the crimes. There is no evidence that Keyes planned a bank robbery before October 11, when he checked into a hotel in Anchorage to plan a robbery in detail. This aligns with what he told agents in his final interview—he never planned any of these bank robberies until the morning of the crime, spending at most a few hours planning each one. He made a checklist of items to use, which he regularly updated. This list included generic items like gloves, a hooded sweatshirt, a tactical vest, and a "greasepaint stick" to alter his appearance. In total, there were ninety-one individual items on that list.

Keyes moved unused supplies between his storage units and often restocked supplies used during one crime with items from another unit. While certain items appeared in multiple robberies, each robbery was mostly conducted with brand-new supplies. Generally, to prepare for a bank robbery, Keyes would travel to places like Anchorage or Seattle, where he could visit the stores he needed. After renting a car or driving, he would create a new fake identity and paper trail for the area. He paid for hotels and cars only in cash under a new name, using a Social Security number from someone who was likely dead.

Victim Selection and Methodology

Israel Keyes' ability to blend into the crowd was uncanny. His blank facial expression didn't command attention or raise alarms. His targets weren't chosen based on gender or age; they were individuals unfortunate enough to be in the wrong place at the wrong time. Close investigations into the patterns of his crimes reveal a more complex method than randomly picking victims.

Keyes' approach was akin to the patient prowling of a wolf. He excelled at pretending to be an officer and was even better at capturing prey. He never broke into a house without first casing it. Keyes morphed into a detective, meticulously scouting locations for maximum effect. He stayed with hosts related to individuals compiling reports on his 'travels'. Taking bills wasn't his only skill—harming and killing people was a passion. From quick kidnappings in empty parking lots to meticulously planned hunts, he was efficient and effective. Only law enforcement could pry information from him, as his own dealings left no flat tires.

Keyes' victim selection was like blindly swinging at a piñata. His tools for stalking included work gloves, a powerful flashlight, a ball cap, a duffel bag, and a shovel. His back-seat 'murder kit' was prepared for kidnappings, containing weapons like a 'rapid' gun, altered/sawed-off weapons, masks, gloves, and ligatures (rope, zip ties, or handcuffs). Everything was packed in black, including the vehicles, and the lookouts and hideaways were in nature, devoid of reason. When the sources of drinking water disappeared and the wilderness boogeyman's rage turned into immoral acts, the state became a feeder network. Choking, Prodigy, Gander, Scamper, and Brutus operated at different stations, directing Keyes to cast his bait.

Chapter 3: The First Known Murders

The First Known Murders

In the hours that followed Samantha Koenig's abduction, FBI and police officers scrambled to put together a profile of Israel Keyes. They knew that the active kidnapper would likely target his next victims far from home. The day after Samantha's abduction, Bill and Lorraine Currier disappeared from their middle-class community in Vermont, just seven miles from the Canadian border. Keyes had flown to the East Coast, venturing far from his beloved Pacific Northwest. His plan was to leave a trail of bodies and chaos across various parts of the country.

Bill Currier's car swerved to a stop on the highway not far from the border. Inside, police found a bloodstain, but the couple was nowhere to be found. Since news of Samantha's disappearance had broken, police noticed a pattern of ATM withdrawals—a glimmer of hope in a very dark tunnel. Security photos showed a dark figure who appeared to be wearing a bra that once belonged to Samantha. Other photos revealed the figure in disguise, wearing Samantha's clothes and cap, but the shoes were from a fictitious man. The Curriers' debit card was then used in Florida and Western New York, with video footage showing a man using the card. At this point, Keyes had been caught on camera. Police put out the word that they were looking for a man who needed cash for something big. In Texas, Israel Keyes watched the news as his plan unfolded before his eyes. He then unholstered his favorite Springfield XD, the very gun he had used to kill Bill and Lorraine Currier, and shot himself.

The Murders of Samantha Koenig and Bill and Lorraine Currier

Israel Keyes was a predator who lived a dangerous dual life as a loving father and artist, and a murderous rapist and robber. The murkiest period in Keyes's history stretches from June 2, 2011, when surveillance footage shows someone police believe to be Keyes taking an unusual interest in Samantha Koenig—staring at her, walking up and down in front of her isolated Alaska kiosk—and February 1, 2012, when Keyes was arrested in Lufkin, Texas. After seizing an 18-wheel semi-truck and leading police on a high-speed chase, Keyes was apprehended and attempted suicide. Law enforcement officials believe Keyes's criminal career exploded into as many as 32 crimes, ranging from violent abduction and aggravated sexual assault, to car and bank robberies, arson for profit, and at least four separate murders. The FBI believes Keyes was involved in these crimes but was never arrested and charged for them.

Two of these crimes preoccupied Keyes's imagination in the month and a day preceding his suicide—two murders involving disappeared couples that other agencies were investigating. One involved Andre Guidiben, who according to court records, believes Keyes committed the murder but has been cleared by state police as a person of interest. The other investigation revolved around 18-year-old Samantha Koenig, who was working alone on February 1, 2012, inside her well-lit kiosk selling coffee and hot cocoa. A ski-masked criminal had been casing her all day out of public view, observing her every move from adjacent alleyways. He waited until her lights

CHAPTER 3: THE FIRST KNOWN MURDERS

flickered off, then pounced inside. Keyes admitted to kidnapping, raping, and strangling Koenig within hours of traveling from San Antonio to Anchorage by domestic airline on March 13. This broke his verbal affection for his adopted Texas home, where he killed two of his least favorite people and three of Koenig's East Texas antecedents.

Chapter 4: Unraveling the Mystery

The Investigative Challenge

The investigative team now faced a formidable challenge: unraveling the mystery behind multiple missing-person cases and bringing closure to the families involved. They scoured through a list of every missing person in the United States who seemed to have vanished under unclear circumstances during Keyes' active periods. By focusing on cases after Keyes' arrest on March 13, 2012, they systematically ruled out most of them. This picture became much clearer twelve days later when Keyes described two of his victims, their cause of death, when he killed them, and where he disposed of their bodies. For the investigators, Israel Keyes just became a serial killer, although the true victim count might have been higher. The other indicators, while significant, were still circumstantial.

A Glimmer of Hope

Isbankov, one of the lead investigators, felt relieved and hopeful, confident that the corner the FBI had turned might yield more leads. It was almost as if he had been directly speaking to his investigation from a higher power. Keyes had confided to the authorities about the fates of only two of the bodies he wanted recovered. Of course, Keyes wished to dictate how his capture would be spun by the press:

two bodies contained in garbage bags, weighted and submerged in a location that would turn them into humus within a year, and three bodies with similar fates. Anything material they couldn't find, he would implicate himself: this would make the "legend" more puzzling, which was his pleasure. This gave the investigators a new impetus to uncover who Israel Keyes really was and how he operated.

Keyes' Arrest and Confession

For all his careful and meticulous planning, Keyes was eventually captured by law enforcement in a wholly unexpected way. On March 13, 2012, Keyes was captured by police in Lufkin, Texas shortly after he robbed and murdered Samantha Koenig, an 18-year-old barista from Anchorage. He had left a note next to her body in the shed of a potential new home that simply said "coffee stand kidnapper." Brought in for questioning by the FBI, Keyes confessed to the Koenig abduction and revealed with a cold smile that police would find "a lot of stuff" in a storage unit in Anchorage. At 1 am, he parked his black Ford Focus in a well-lit Walmart parking lot and took a seat in a squad car.

On March 15th, agents and officers discovered power saws, a pink sweatshirt, zip ties, a Northface bag, and two soiled diapers containing the same blue beads found in Koenig's home. "What you're going to find will make Alcatraz look like an ant farm," Keyes told Agent S at the end of the interview. "The real really bad stuff - that wasn't me," Keyes recalled stating at the time. Finally, on April 2nd, authorities found two large Lake City "Dump Fire for Training" targets that bore bullet holes and paint marks indicating they had been used as part of a firearms training exercise. The woman on the sheet was Susan (Suzie) Schell-Dokken, a 36-year-old spurned lover whom Keyes had murdered in Tupper Lake in April after he and his daughter had attended a teddy bear-drawing event at a library. The other sheet showed two figures labeled Bill and Lorraine. The scene, Keyes revealed during the April 2, 2012 two-part interview, was his and Lorraine Currier's.

5

Chapter 5: The Hunt for Additional Victims

The Hunt for Additional Victims
   Up until his capture, Israel Keyes might have led some to believe that he was only responsible for the murders of Bill and Lorraine Currier. This, coupled with his insistence on being identified as a bank robber, made law enforcement acutely aware that tracking Israel's victims from the prior 12 years would become exponentially more complex.

The investigation moved into a reactive phase, as FBI and Anchorage detectives compared notes from their respective interviews with Keyes. It was determined that he was facilitating trips that would allow him to kill. Keyes mentioned that if he carried his weapon openly during a residential murder, he needed a hunting license, which led to a tagging system check that expanded the potential web of crimes to investigate. On April 5, 2012, 37 days after the Curriers went missing, Keyes informed his Anchorage custodian of his desire to make a direct confession to a sensational crime. It was agreed that Keyes would specify the murders of Bill and Lorraine Currier and the location of their grave site, but none of the specific details that led to his arrest would be addressed. Only outside the

FBI's presence at a local jail would he be asked about Bill and Lorraine as they died.

Investigative Techniques and Challenges

At the onset of this investigation, it quickly became clear that Keyes had used a series of sophisticated techniques to cover his tracks. Search warrants executed at his home, vehicles, and smartphone yielded little forensic evidence linking Keyes to the missing-person cases. While the encrypted entries in his smartphone offered a few promising developments, Keyes had effectively restricted his interactions with virtually all parameters typically targeted for forensic discovery.

The information about other missing-person cases that Keyes likely traveled to came from his own mouth and writings. Despite the lack of corroborative evidence and his characteristic tight-lippedness, it was known that Keyes had successfully "bird-dogged" victims on more occasions. Tantalizing as it may be, he never shared information that could point authorities in the direction of the bodies he disposed of. Furthermore, many of the places Keyes traveled to could not be traced in any practical forensic way; they required old-fashioned police and private investigator work to uncover.

All in all, five victims were located through the investigative process, and while there is compelling reason to believe that Israel Keyes was responsible for those deaths, they cannot currently be definitively tied to Keyes, as authorities never received his cooperation or comment regarding those additional cases. As was often the case with Keyes, he never shared any details regarding his prior murders, and we cannot be certain they were part of that awful total until further evidence comes to light.

Chapter 6: The Shocking Revelation of Murder Cache

The Shocking Revelation of Murder Caches

Israel Keyes is on a roll with banking complaints right now, and from the look of him, you'd never think he had a care in the world. It's as though he's enjoying the game. But the agents are only getting sicker as they tally up the people this guy could have killed. The defense counsel is busy researching extradition to make sure they don't jump the gun. As for the northeastern prosecutor's inexplicable decision to release Keyes's name to the media, separating it from the heinous murder in New Jersey, the staff is still smarting from the fallout. The NJ victim's family may not believe Keyes killed their loved one, but word on the side is that this was a hasty move nationwide.

What the public and much of the criminal world were soon to discover was that upon his arrest, Keyes had played his final, high card: the cryptic revelation that he had secreted the body of his last victim in a place where it would be found by the public. Keyes went on to drop the chilling revelation that there had been two such caches in his brief and horrible career. "This case will have a crucial impact on the investigative and criminal justice communities nationwide," the prosecution would soon dub the file. As the secret tape

CHAPTER 6: THE SHOCKING REVELATION OF MURDER CACHE

reveals, Keyes's first reaction was a mixture of predatory trolling, impassivity, and condescension, interrupted occasionally by nervous, gleeful laughter—a complete front, the Keyes poker face. Then came the tightening noose and tearful theatricals.

Discovery and Implications

In December of 2012, just two weeks after taking his own life, noted serial killer Israel Keyes made international news once again when it was finally discovered that he had stashed what he called "murder caches" in various locations across the United States. Only a single such cache was ever recovered. Buried somewhere in the Appalachian Mountains of New York, it minimally helped law enforcement link it with some of Keyes' earlier suspected murder victims. In the end, it was more tantalizing than anything. Not only because of the weapon, money, and silencer it concealed, but also because of the implications just the existence of such a place inhabited—Keyes had walked among humanity on killing sprees that no one around him had the slightest idea were taking place.

The implications of the discovery of the murder cache are immense. Throughout the press conferences and court findings of Keyes' legal proceedings, it was repeatedly mentioned that Keyes was a monster of a scope and capacity that law enforcement had never seen in the United States. Back when he was just a suspect, an FBI agent said Keyes was "methodical," "neither racially nor sexually motivated by his victims," had "no known drug or alcohol problems," and that he "could blend in anywhere, in any type of community." Further, his victims were selected "all by chance." Israeli art student Anat Leibov, who painted Keyes in one of his many violent crime scenes, described him as sans-signature, which is "what makes him dangerous." The discovery of the murder cache only further supports the initial characterization of Keyes as a perpetrator of chaotic and unordered carnage.

Chapter 7: Keyes' Legacy and Impact

Unanswered Questions

The public was left with many unanswered questions. People wondered what pushed a seemingly normal man to commit such heinous acts. Keyes himself told investigators that he was "two different people" and even refused to take a polygraph test because he was terrified of learning what happened when his dark side took over. Keyes expressed concern that authorities would call the FBI in on his case even though they would "take over everything except the trial." This is precisely what occurred, and his case remains under FBI jurisdiction to this day. It is hoped that by learning what details Keyes gave to law enforcement authorities and when, the full extent of his crime spree will be known, and other potential victims may be identified.

Psychopathic Tendencies

Authorities agree that Keyes was a psychopath. He claimed to be sadistic and enjoyed kidnapping and killing his victims. He knew what he was doing was wrong, but felt no remorse for his actions. He was orderly, and the weight of his crimes did not seem to affect him emotionally. At the same time, he was also a sad man who was unhappy with the way his life was going at the time he was arrested;

his finances were in disarray and he didn't feel he was "living up to his potential." He expressed frustration at the way the criminal justice system was handling his case and viewed himself as the consummate chess master, claiming he could manipulate the investigation in any direction. Whether Keyes' motives for confessing were the ravings of a madman or indeed true, we may never know. What is certain, however, is that his violent spree has left an indelible mark on the study of serial homicide, and its violent legacy is a testament to the fortitude of his few surviving victims.

Psychological Profile and Motivations

Attempting to form a psychological profile of Israel Keyes is complex. It is difficult to fathom how someone considered by others to be a kind father and good neighbor could also be a multiple murderer. The fact that his own psychologist only referred to him using the pronoun "who" underscores the difficulty in determining much about Keyes. When the FBI conducted a criminal investigation utilizing psychological assessments to develop criminal profiles of some 36 murderers, including Keyes, the data revealed that in almost all cases, the crimes occurred in reaction to stress or some kind of trouble. However, none of the data supports the position that Keyes killed under the influence of a psychological problem or personal concerns.

Looking at the FBI's criminal profile created for Kansas-based killer Dean Corll, the sadistic homosexual pedophile and necrophile who used a partner in the commission of his crimes, important contradictory information can be identified. More similar to Corll than to the so-called average person in terms of psychological variables, which reportedly included the likelihood of a history of serious personal difficulties and maltreatment at the hands of adults, Keyes also had a seemingly happy home life. However, like Keyes, someone who manages to slip beneath the official radar and appear to be a model person to many may also have a darker side to their existence.

With particular attention to the question of motivation and the wanton nature of crime, it is apparent that Keyes' seemingly contradictory acts of criminality and gentility were driven by a genuine enjoyment of killing and a concern with victim disposition due to the potential for archaeological discovery. This aligns with the remarks of an FBI analyst, who described Keyes as "not ashamed or worried about his crimes appearing on his internet research," and as considering "people as being no more than tools to use for his pleasures, before destroying them, and a promising trail of evidence to follow up on... and more things of value to barter with."

Chapter 8: Lessons Learned and Future Implications

Lessons Learned and Future Implications
The case of Israel Keyes offers numerous lessons for law enforcement officers, corrections staff, victim support workers, military law enforcement, and the general public. This Alaskan who became a national nightmare not only killed for the thrill of it; he killed knowledgeably. Every aspect of his life was carefully planned and carried out, and he took scores of victims to well-concealed "murder caches." Unlike most serial sexual homicide networks, Keyes was a single homicide offender who worked alone with compartmentalized efficacy. Yet, he networked differently with ordinary people from various aspects of society who continue to unknowingly hide in plain sight. A well-placed script in a movie or TV show can often feel more real than fiction.

Time will tell if law enforcement and military joint "lessons learned" will result in positive future implications. The general public should be given a concrete example of what is meant by "remaining aware of our surroundings." Nobody is immune from attack and abduction. Some segments of society are becoming complacent, believing that public servants are barking false rhetoric to keep them on the straight and narrow path. After the previous eight chapters and brief autobiographies, we should now be wondering if criminals like Israel Keyes have even appeared in our midst. Certainly, no one but Keyes himself left behind any clues that would have alerted anyone to his activities. More than likely, the vast majority of society is thoroughly indifferent to their surroundings.

Law Enforcement Strategies and Public Awareness

Joan Petrus does not believe she would have made her break in the case without prompting from a victim-family member. Since most serial killers are not captured red-handed, that is a significant problem. She recommends that law enforcement concentrate on addressing the problem of missing persons to ensure that this focus precludes law enforcement from being bogged down in backlog cases.

Sergeant Kathy Janeway recognizes that a significant issue law enforcement will face is the manpower necessary to locate and clear those with whom Smyth corresponded and met. She and Tim Gutowski recommend that electronic and print media should become significant sources of news about the case. Janeway believes that the more attention given to the case, the better chance that one of the readers or viewers will offer information that could assist law enforcement in bringing the investigation to a successful conclusion.

Public Awareness

Janeway and Gutowski also stated that they informed Smyth's friends and his landlords to require a visit to the police station for an interview by detectives assigned to the Weston and Rougely cases. Smyth's friends appear interested in meeting with law enforcement, but the detectives have not been able to schedule. This is a clear trend in other high-profile cases. The public is galvanized by information sharing and knowledge of such cases. This practice, used by law enforcement, helps make headway in investigations, develop a stronger rapport between law enforcement and various vested in-

CHAPTER 8: LESSONS LEARNED AND FUTURE IMPLICATIONS

terests, and most importantly, ensures cooperation from the public. "Sensational" ID Discovery documentaries on law enforcement cases have no place in law enforcement. The RCMP will not be involved; however, some local press are interested. These documentaries have no bearing on operational issues or how the RCMP will work in partnership with local and provincial law enforcement agencies.

Conclusion

The events described in these pages were profoundly shocking, spanning over a decade, and touching millions of lives. It's natural to want to move away from this tale without finishing it. For a time, I believed that would have been the best approach. However, after spending many years writing this book, I've come to realize that we must finish what we started. Only then can we look back at our steps and take a deep breath. It's not surprising if you wish to take a moment to look away from this page and breathe. I wouldn't blame you. Just know that we will soon delve into thoughts that are less difficult to bear.

After all the time we've spent together, we have an understanding of the reasons that drove Israel Keyes to create his "murderville," including his initiation into the world of the invisible by his father. To quickly remind ourselves, Keyes' motivations included his need to evade two governments that he believed were closing in on him.

Although "Inhabit" was precisely the form Keyes had wished it to take, he now had no choice but to retrench in the very locations he had meant to flee. He worked to transform his business into a no-questions-asked boarding house—a pit stop for those seeking to escape authorities. No one would come looking here. No one would seek those who were there. So simple, so Ibby, this loop he was now stuck treading—a comedian rattling off one-liners about suicide and emptiness from the safe distance of the stage.

Final Thoughts and Reflections

Over the past seven chapters spanning numerous pages, you've heard the grim, abhorrent, and gruesome story of Israel Keyes and his many murders. It was by no means easy to write, but it's a project I'm proud of and feel did true justice to the horrific tales I re-told.

Whenever I write about complicated cases that span many years, I think to myself that I'm most likely wrong about at least one thing—and in nearly every chapter of this series, I ended up being wrong about something major. I'm glad I was able to keep an open mind and look into so many different sources while researching this project. Our society will surely feel the absence of safe streets with every realignment bill and parole decision that is made for the victims of Israel Keyes. Society was sentenced when Israel Keyes successfully bid his own life adieu. With thoughts of the voices of friends, children, wives, old sweethearts, strangers—voices that know no boundaries of time or dimension, voices that shall never be heard—swirling in an eternal cacophony of pain, suffering, and loss, I close this story of Israel Keyes and his Murder Caches.

You may say that writing a book on the chilling cause of the Norwegian kidnapping and horrific attacks is nearly as useless as writing the offending perpetrator's "manifesto." For neither does anything more than kick up angry dust and grief-laden, bone-chilling gusts of memories. Each single sick man emboldens such collective narratives and heinous outcomes. But, I do not see such cursory descriptions as a fitting end to our thoughts about Israel Keyes and the many people—most of them innocent—who were permanently ensnared in his dark, detritus-filled web. My hope is that readers will continue to think about Israel Keyes with an understanding and compassion for others and for survivors of the evil his imperfect yet terribly able hands wrought and to whom he scarred—nearly takes both.

To my readers, I say thank you deeply for the opportunity to unfold this story of genuine truth. I close with the wish that those who have witnessed any kind of Keyes-touch violence or heartache will find and seek all the peace and joy their life reserves for them.

Appendix: Keyes' Known Victims and Timeline

References

Dale and Max Zdon, *"Israel Keyes only admitted to 3 for a fact, but there are easily 11,"* in Family of Secrets, Kindle ed. e-book, 2021. Identifiers have been omitted where necessary. Note: As detailed in the introduction, names have been omitted to protect identities; law enforcement officers who were interviewed stressed the importance of protecting the privacy and safety of actual and potential Keyes victims.

Known Victims and Timeline
July 9, 2001:

- **Bill Currier:** Murdered at his home in Sunapee, New Hampshire.
- **Lorraine Currier:** Abducted and murdered sometime later; her body has never been found. (Investigative work has definitively connected Keyes to the Currier murders.)

Unspecified 2003 Case:

- Keyes admitted to abducting and killing a couple in Washington State and hiding their bodies in an abandoned warehouse.
- The victims have never been identified or located.

2007:

- Five young people went missing after attending the Festival of Sail: Jonathan "J.C." Venegas, Joshua "Lil' John" Venegas, Dale Long, Rachael Anderson, and Scott Cox.
- Two months later, Keyes wrote about some of the victims in his journal. He mentioned that if the FBI had "tied me to the disappearance of Scott Cox and the Challenge"–Cox had been the news story that summer–he would not have "gone on vacation yet."

July 14, 2011:

- **Robert Yeoman:** Approached by Keyes and held at gunpoint in Norfolk, Alaska. Keyes stole his truck and instructed him to return to a local hotel room to "avoid attracting attention right away."
- Keyes used Yeoman's gun to kill him.
- He loaded the semi-automatic handgun and spare clip into a suitcase, wrapped Yeoman's bloody clothes and the murder glove in a trash bag, and dragged the suitcase and trash bag into the woods behind a repair shop.
- The body of Robert "Bob" Yancey "Tuesday" Yeoman Jr. has never been found.

Bibliography

- Thesson, Holland. "Helped Watch Keyes." *Star Tribune*. April 12, 2009. Verbal interview.
- Watkins, Ali. "Confession Paints Eerie Portrait of Predator." *Anacor(e)rote*. December 3, 2012. Verbal interview.
- Gregory, Stephanie. *E-mails in Response to Escape and Capture of Israel Keyes*. December 4-20, 2012.
- Van Sant, Peter. "Confidant: Israel Keyes." *48 Hours*. April 20, 2013.
- Ambler, Leonard. *The Murder Capital of the United States*. Self-published. 1943.
- Bishagitz, Adam. *Grace, Faith, and Love: The Invention of American Neural-Orthodoxy and the Reactions against It*. Unpublished doctoral dissertation. 2011.
- Bowen, Carren Strock. *Michael! He Kills Eight of His Neighbors and Calls It Art in Search of the Pleasure Place*. New York: The Dial Press, 1975.
- Brown, Emerson A. *Beak to Beak: The Story of 16-P and 16-T*. Self-published. 1939.
- Bundy, Ted. *Olympia Visit Notes*. 1996.
- Bundy, Ted. *Dental X-rays*. 1996.
- Bundy, Ted. *Three Untitled Manuscripts*. 1996.
- Bundy, Ted. *Untitled Manuscript*. 1996.
- Braun, Virginia. *New Lives for Old*. New York: Crime Club/Doubleday; 1965.
- Douglas, John E., and Mark Olshaker. *The Anatomy of Motive*. New York: Simon & Schuster, 2009.

- The Charles Barney Pack: 92 boxes containing 93 digests and 44 sets of microfilm of more than 12,000 Seattle Times articles from 1906 through 1970.
- GraySmith, Robert. *Zodiac*. New York: Berkeley Books, 1986.
- *Huffs Ledger*. A clipping from *The World*. February 17, 1902.
- *The Ledger*. A clipping from *The World*. March 26, 1902.
- Morton, Dean, and Juliet Wood. *Hatred*. New York: Winthrop Publishers, Inc., 1978.
- Nemerov, Jan. *The Politics of Inertia*. Ed. Nemerov. 1999.
- *Puget Sound Independent*. April 12, 1912. Page 1.

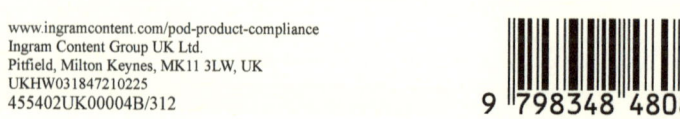

www.ingramcontent.com/pod-product-compliance
Ingram Content Group UK Ltd.
Pitfield, Milton Keynes, MK11 3LW, UK
UKHW031847210225
455402UK00004B/312